Seasons of the Soul

SUE JOHNSON

For my children.

ACKNOWLEDGEMENTS:

Scriptures taken from The Voice TM. Copyright © 2012 by Ecclesia Bible Society.
Used by permission. All rights reserved.

Scriptures taken from the Amplified Bible, Copyright © 2015 by Lockman Foundation.
Used by permission.

Scriptures taken from the Holy Bible, New International Version, NIV. Copyright 1973, 1978, 1984,
2011 by Biblica, Inc. TM Used by permission of Zondervan. All rights reserved.

Scriptures taken from The Message. Copyright A 1993, 1994, 1995, 1996, 2000, 2001 ,2002.
Used by permission of NavPress Publishing Group.

Images courtesy of Unsplash, Pexels, Sue Johnson, Sarah Johnson and James Johnson.
Cover photo by Chris Lawton on Unsplash.

Layout and design Copyright © Designer & Illustrator Sarah Johnson.

Contents

A Christmas Memory ...

A little over 50 years ago, a young girl visited an Old People's home with her parents to sing Christmas Carols, and to tell them again, the wonderful story of the baby in a manger. They had been many times before, but today would create a memory that would last a lifetime ...

On the front row sat Jack, and Lizzie thought he must be ancient. His tired eyes were sad and downcast, his skin was crumpled like scrunched up greaseproof paper. His shirtsleeves were rolled up above knobbly elbows revealing skinny arms; over-sized hands, once so strong and hardworking, lay twisted and stiff in his lap, which was peppered with ash from cigarettes. Although the singing was lively, the weary feet erupting from Jack's carpet slippers, had no tapping left in them.

As the festive service progressed, Jack fumbled in his waistcoat pocket, pulling out a battered leather pouch of tobacco, along with a flimsy square of paper. Carefully balancing a dented metal lighter on the arm of his chair, he set about rolling himself a cigarette. Lizzie had seen her grandfather perform this ritual and knew how it was supposed to go, but it soon became obvious that Jack's fingers didn't have the same flexibility as her Grandad's.

Her fascinated gazing was interrupted by her father's voice announcing that she was going to sing her favourite carol, then and now, Away in a Manger. Standing to her feet as the pianist hammered out the introduction, she turned her attention to the rest of the room and began ...

Away in a manger, no crib for a bed,
The little Lord Jesus lay down His sweet head ...

Most of the residents closed their eyes, nodding in time to the music, their own memories of this ageless melody mingling with the rise and fall of Lizzie's voice. But then, just as the cattle were lowing, she spotted Jack and his cigarette. He had managed to tease a pinch of tobacco from the pouch and place it at one end of the paper. Now he was rolling it, not without considerable difficulty, and she marveled that even his tongue seemed shriveled up as he held it to his lips. Trembling, bony fingers fashioned the paper into a somewhat crushed cigarette, then he popped one end into his mouth and reached for the lighter.

With horror, Lizzie saw that Jack had put the tobacco filled end of the cigarette into his mouth, and as he brought the lighter closer and closer to the other end, it dawned on her what would happen next. She knew she must keep singing, but she couldn't look away.

At last, Jack's hand-eye co-ordination came together, the lighter connected with the paper just a couple of inches from the end of his pointy nose. The flame began travelling towards his face. Jack's eyes widened, and gradually crossed as he followed its progress until, just before it would surely set him on fire, it reached the tobacco and halted. Jack puffed furiously, sending up clouds of smoke. He closed his eyes; satisfaction finally replacing panic on his timeworn face, but then he took the last inch from his mouth, the bit with most of the tobacco in it, and stubbed it out. Lizzie was so relieved; Jack would not go up in flames today!

Some memories do indeed, last a lifetime.

And some prayers are ageless too, like the final verse of the song that Lizzie sang that evening so long ago.

🙏 **Be near me Lord Jesus, I ask You to stay**
Close by me forever, and love me, I pray.
Bless all the dear children in Your tender care,
And take us to heaven to live with You there.

Still waiting?

So, were you thrilled with all your Christmas presents then, or did the annual gaffs make another appearance?

You know the ones! There's the aunt, or someone you haven't seen for ages, who sends a jumper that's way too big, or a DVD that you already have 2 copies of! Did Santa get it right, or were you a little disappointed?

What about God - does He ever disappoint? When you look back over the year that is fast fading, how will you feel? Did God show up for you this year, or does it feel like He let you down? Let's be honest, although there have been some days of celebration, God hasn't always responded to our prayers the way we'd have liked Him to.

It's a strange thing to say, but Jesus, when He lived on earth, sometimes left people feeling disappointed. For example, a man who became known as "The Rich Young Ruler" asked Jesus how he could get eternal life, and he was disappointed with the answer. Jesus' family wanted Him to behave a certain way, but they were disappointed, perhaps embarrassed even when He refused to comply with their expectations. The royalty of the day wanted Him to put on a show, to impress and entertain them with miracles and signs; they too were disappointed. And even the disciples, Jesus' closest friends, sometimes felt let down by Him - like the time when they thought they were drowning and Jesus lay snoring in the boat.

What are you asking God to do for you? You need to know that His love for you is unquestionable, that He sees things you cannot see, that even though it may seem like He's sleeping on the job right now, He's with you, and He's working things out.

"Let all that I am wait quietly before God, for my hope is in Him."
Psalm 62:5

As yet untouched?

I know, you either love it or hate it. I've just had some for breakfast so I guess I must come in the "love it" camp. But I had to scrape out the jar this morning, which is never so good because the thing I love most about Marmite ... is taking the first scoop out of a new jar! There's something about the smooth, shiny, untouchedness (is that even a word?) that makes me feel ever so slightly excited when I remove the lid of a new jar for the very first time. Odd I know, but there you go.

And this morning I have a similar sense but on a different scale as we launch ourselves into another year. It stretches out ahead of us like freshly fallen snow, as yet unmarked by the footprints that will inevitably be left as we journey through each day as it comes. And in my heart stirs an excitement, an anticipation, a thirst for a deeper, closer, more vibrant relationship with the Lord of the years; the hope of seeing more of His kingdom breaking out in my life, and the lives of those I love and with whom I serve.

"I am not yet as God wants me to be. I have not yet reached that goal, but I continue trying to reach it and to make it mine. Christ wants me to do that, which is the reason He made me His. Brothers and sisters, I know that I have not yet reached that goal, but there is one thing I always do. Forgetting the past and straining toward what is ahead, I keep trying to reach the goal and get the prize for which God called me, through Christ, to the life above."
Philippians 3:12-14

Father in heaven, thank you for this new day, this New Year; I invite You to do a new thing in me as it unfolds. Keep me pressing forwards, pushing deeper into You. May Your kingdom come in my life, yes, let Your will be done. Amen

Mistaken identity ...

It's over once more! And I'm a bit sad to be honest. One of the things I love about Christmas is sitting by our tree early in the morning, reading my Bible and praying by the light of the 148 twinkling miniature bulbs that nestle among the red tinsel and golden baubles. But yesterday, when I got in from work, I knew the time had come to dismantle the trappings of Christmas, to hoover into the corners once again and to try to get the sticky tape off the window frame!

In an effort to make the task less melancholy, I resorted to turning on the telly and found one final Christmas film to keep me company. It involved a case of mistaken identity. A little boy crept from his bed late one night just before Christmas, and, from his vantage point on the landing, to his horror, he saw Santa kissing his Mummy in front of the fireplace in the living room below. There followed an hour or so of this previously "good as gold" child being as naughty as he could be in an effort to protect his parent's marriage by stopping Santa coming to his house again, only to discover in the dying moments of the film that Santa was, of course, his own Daddy. (Oops, I hope that hasn't burst anyone's bubble!)

Mistaken identity. Had the child got close he would have seen and known who it was, but from a distance it was impossible to tell.

Jesus once asked His followers who people thought He was. From a distance, some had concluded that He was John the Baptist, some thought He was a re-incarnation of Elijah, Jeremiah or one of the other Old Testament prophets. But Peter walked with Jesus up close, and Peter knew this amazing truth:

 "You are the Messiah, the Son of the living God." Matthew 16:16

Who do YOU think He is? And are you basing your opinion on distant observations, or by getting up close?

Had the little boy in the film known who Santa really was, he would never have pushed him away.

God of heaven, I want to get to know You better, to be so close to You that I won't be mistaken about what You're like. As a new year unfolds, please open my eyes so that I can see You as You really are. Expand my knowledge and understanding, and give me the courage to make it known, that You are still the One who saves. Amen.

Pressed down, shaken together and running over ...

There are those who would never voluntarily give anything to anyone; there are those who give only what they feel obliged to. But then there are those who give above and beyond any reasonable expectation, and they do it with a smile, deriving pleasure from the giving, adding blessing upon blessing to those who are receiving.

If tight-fisted is at zero and generous is at ten, I wonder what you would score? I thank God for those people in my life who score a big fat ten!

And what of God?

"Your love, Lord, reaches to the heavens,
Your faithfulness to the skies.
Your righteousness is like the highest
mountains, Your justice like the great deep.
You, Lord, preserve both people and animals.
How priceless is Your unfailing love, O God!
People take refuge in the shadow of Your wings.
They feast on the abundance of Your house; You
give them drink from Your river of delights.
For with You is the fountain of life; in Your light
we see light." Psalm 36:5-9

Father, I thank You for the people in my life who show me something of Your love by their generosity. Pour blessings into their lives, and continue to shape them in the likeness of Your Son, who gave everything for me. Thank You that You continually open Your hand and shower me with good things. Thank You for Your faithfulness, for the protection that is to be found in the shelter of Your wings, for the unconditional love that knows no limit and from which there is no escape. Thank You that Your grace is enough, always. Amen

He is here ...

It was minus 6 degrees when I left the cottage early one Sunday morning. The sky was a clear brilliant blue and an icy blanket of stillness wrapped itself around me. I made my way gingerly out of the unfamiliar driveway and eased the car round skating rink corners and up hills like ski-slopes. For a while I was unsure that I had found the right road across the wintry Dales and begun to wonder if I had made this rather dodgy journey in vain. But then, just as I was thinking that maybe I should turn back, I spotted the place of my pilgrimage. Rather closer to the edge that I would have liked, I pulled the car onto a narrow patch of crunchy undergrowth and stopped the engine. Getting out, I breathed a sigh of relief that hung in the cold air around me; I had finally at arrived at the spot I'd been wanting to revisit for months.

But what now? Last time I was here the presence of God was tangible, His voice as clear then as the sky was now. I shivered, waiting for God to arrive, not quite sure He had this appointment in His diary. In any case, it seemed to me like He was late.

In the waiting, I looked around me, and suddenly, I was struck by the awesome beauty that I could see all around me. Over to my right was Ingleborough; it looked miniature now on the distant horizon, but when I had climbed it a couple of years ago it had seemed huge. In front of me, the windy single-track road ducked between the ridges of the Dale, weaving a pattern with the becks that burbled their way over shiny rocks down to the river.

Their journey would continue to the far away sea, that even now, glistened in the early morning sunshine. Beyond the bay rose the majestic hills of Cumbria in ever darker layers, all capped with freshly fallen snow. Time stood still, and as I began to slowly take in all that I could see, I was struck by the weight of an immense silence. With the exception of the occasional grouse call, there was no sound up here at all, nothing. The emptiness seemed as big as the panorama before me; it found an echo in my soul. And now, I found I had very little to say.

After who knows how long, from over my shoulder, I caught a glimpse of a wispy cloud in the otherwise pure blue sky, and all at once this cloud displayed within it all the colours of the rainbow. I wrote in my journal, "He is here."

There was no trumpet fanfare, no whistles or bells, no surge of emotion or gush of tears, just the absolute certainty that God was all around me; the evidence was indisputable.

Eventually, God spoke just seven words to me. He said, "My silence does not indicate my absence." And surrounded by this raw beauty, that had already challenged my perspectives, I knew it was true.

Does God seem a bit quiet to you these days? Quiet He may be, but His promise is sure –

"I will never abandon you; I will never leave you alone, never."
Hebrews 13:5

New beginnings ...

Every now and then we get the chance to begin again.

I remember taking my maths book to show my teacher one day when I was at Primary School. For some reason I had failed to connect with the lesson that morning and whereas I would normally have returned to my seat feeling quite proud of a neat row of red ticks, on this occasion I was mortified as Mrs Mee first frowned, then shook her head. Next, and with more energy than seemed quite necessary to me, she ripped the page from my book and told me to begin again!

To be fair, new beginnings are not always because we have got things wrong; sometimes it is simply that a season has changed, or that a new opportunity has been created where none existed before.

God has a way of making things new and there is no-one like Him for restoring and mending what is worn out and in need of fixing. When you feel in need of a fresh start, the very best person to go to is Jesus. He alone is able to cleanse and heal you from the past; He alone is able to give you new life.

"When someone becomes a Christian, they become a brand new person inside. They're not the same anymore. A new life has begun!"
2 Corinthians 5:17

Dear Lord Jesus, thank You that You have the power and the authority to give me a new beginning. I ask You to forgive me for the mistakes of the past; I want to be made whole inside; I receive Your promise of new life. Amen

Nothing to say ...

Once, when I was a child, I was told by a lady I barely knew that I had been vaccinated with the same gramophone needle as my father! I guess what she meant was that usually, like my Dad before me, I could find something to say; and it's true, usually I can.

But as I came to pray this morning, I discovered that I'm all talked out.

I was half expecting God to chide me for my lack of concentration, or my inability (perhaps that's unwillingness?) to connect with my own heart in order to pour it out to Him. But no, instead He brought to mind a verse from Psalm 46 ...

 "Be still, and know that I AM God."

So today, praying may not be about words, but about a stillness of heart, and a quiet but unshakable conviction that God is busy being God while I sit peacefully in His presence.

Are you awake?

Now my idea of alarm clocks is that you set it for the time you want to get up, it goes off, you wake up, the day begins - simple! But that's not how it works in our house, oh no. My other half sets the alarm for the time he wants to wake up, it goes off, he sleeps through it, but I don't. Eventually I wake him, gently, and tell him that his alarm has been screaming for the last 12 minutes and isn't it time he got an alarm that woke him instead of me? The frustrating thing is, that when he is awake, he can hear it, just not when he's asleep!

Some sounds are like that - you have to be tuned in to hear them, you have to be listening.

God's voice is a lot like that. He's talking to us, showing us things, calling us to do stuff, leading us, telling us He loves us, but if we're not listening, we miss it all. When you read the bible, listen and ask yourself what God is saying to you. When you pray, don't just talk, listen too. When you take a walk or a drive, when you struggle at work or wrestle with your teenagers, when you sink into a hot bath at the end of one of those days, tune in - let God's voice break through all the other noises …

"Listen and hear My voice; pay attention and hear what I say."
Isaiah 28:23

 Speak to me Father, I'm listening.

What do you say?

How many times when you were little did your Mum start to give you something, and then prompt you with "What do you say?" The correct answer was, of course, "Thank you!" Learning not to take things for granted is an important lesson, and being grateful doesn't always come naturally. Why is it that we find it so much easier to focus on the things that we don't have, rather than all that we do have?

Yesterday, in conversation with a friend, I heard myself say, "Yes, there's so much to smile about." And I don't remember the rest of what we said because it set me thinking. You see, like you, I could easily write a list of reasons to be a bit glum, and let's be honest, there are times when it's appropriate to be sad.

But today, I'm going to choose to say, "Thank you."

Thank You, God, that I'm not hungry, that I could choose what to put on this morning.

Thank You for the people who care for me, children who love me, friends who pray for me.

Thank You that You are good, all the time.

Thank You for the moon, the sea, and leafy lanes.

Thank You for mountains, for grandchildren, for ginger kittens, crispy seaweed, photo albums and memories.

Thank you for Your promise to always be with me.

Psalm 136 is a list of thank you's; what would your list say?

"Give thanks to the Lord, for He is good! His faithful love endures for ever." Psalm 136:1

God is good, always ...

I've just re-written a letter of complaint. My son said the first one was tame, and he may well have been right, so this one is a little bit more fierce! I'm having to let a very large company know that I am extremely unhappy about the way they have handled something. I'm not confident that I will get a response that I will be satisfied with, but I do feel a bit better for having had a bit of a go.

I don't usually make a lot of fuss, not so as you'd notice anyway, although I'm not bad at having a good moan to myself when things are not going the way I think they should. Don't you think it's odd that companies have a Complaints Procedure, and yet they seem so unwilling to actually do anything when you have a complaint?

But what about God? What do I do when He does something I don't approve of, or perhaps He doesn't do what I think He should, or at least not when I think He should, and certainly not how I think He should? Or perhaps what He does costs me too much? Does God have a complaint's procedure?

 *"I call to the Lord for help, I plead with Him. I bring Him my complaints. I tell Him all my troubles. When I am ready to give up, He knows what I should do." Psalm 142:1-3*

You and I will not always like what happens to us, or to those we know and love, and God knows that. So, His invitation to us is to talk to Him about it; if you have a complaint, tell Him. God can handle our disappointment, and our disapproval come to that. His response is not guaranteed to be what you want it to be, but sometimes He will help us to understand things from a different perspective; sometimes we will learn to trust Him more deeply than we have before; sometimes it will be enough, just knowing that He is there.

But always, God will listen to our complaints.

Always, He will respond with love.

And always, God is good.

Heart to heart ...

Hearts have been on the agenda in our family just lately. A month ago, the issue was a heart that had been beating for many years and was struggling to keep going. And then, last week, I heard the most wonderful sound - the heartbeat of a baby yet to be born; amazing!

It has set me thinking ... about my own heart and about the heart of God.

When I talk to God today, will I tell Him what's on my mind, or share what's on my heart? Will I think through carefully what I want to say or let my heart simply overflow? I can use reason to make my thoughts more, well, reasonable, or I can open my heart to the God who loves me and let Him know me as I really am.

I'm not saying that we should by-pass our minds when we pray, after all, according to Luke 10:27 we are to love God with all our mind as well as with all our strength, our soul and our heart. But sometimes I use my mind at the expense of my heart, and sometimes this can cause my heart to become hard.

As I sit here, I suddenly recall a song that I love from many years ago, in which God comes to someone in the night, takes their battered heart in His hands, and holds it there in the warmth until it is soft again.

And what of God's heart? A heart that was broken for love of a people that had rejected Him; a heart generous enough to forgive over and over again. A heart containing love so deep that He has adopted us into His family, engraved us onto the palm of His hand and set about building us a home where we will be able to spend forever with Him.

"He tends His flock like a shepherd; He gathers the lambs in His arms and carries them close to His heart." Isaiah 40:11

Father, I give you my heart today and ask that You hold it in the warmth of Your great love. Thank You that You do not crush a heart that is bruised but rather, You protect it, heal and restore it. I choose to trust You, even on days when I'm confused, and I am comforted to know that through it all, You carry me, and those I love, close to Your heart. Amen

An end, and a beginning ...

Honestly? It had been a rubbish weekend.

It had started promisingly enough – who doesn't like a slap-up meal with friends? And it had been funny really, because most of them weren't actually expecting to go out that night, and when they did, it hadn't been like meals they'd shared before.

As a group, they'd done pretty much everything together for the last, what, almost three years. They'd learned so much, laughed loads and cried a bit too; they'd walked miles and met some amazing people, lots of them quite needy really, but they were learning how to make a difference, how to be less selfish – though some of them were struggling with that more than others!

After dinner, which they decided was probably the most succulent piece of roast lamb they'd had in a very long time, one of them suggested they go for a walk. It was odd; the atmosphere was strangely tense that night, and as they wandered through the trees a heaviness seemed to settle over them, though some thought it was the effect of all the bread and the wine!

Few of them were certain exactly what happened next. The pale and gentle light of the waning moon suddenly gave way to the blazing torches of an angry mob and you could almost smell the danger in the cold night air as the friends were circled by the dark shadows of an agitated crowd. There was a scuffle, raised voices, confusion, the flash of a blade and a wrongful arrest. Hearts thumped violently; breath came in painful gasps as most of them fled; self-preservation is a powerful force.

By the time they realized what had happened, it was too late anyway. Some were seized by regret, others tormented by shame as over the next 24 hours, terrible events unfolded. Others felt the crushing weight of loss as they witnessed the cruel, icy grasp of hatred and jealousy tightening, robbing the One they loved of life itself.

That night, it had felt like the end, but as a new week dawned two days later, the pain and trauma of that tumultuous weekend was overtaken by a new, almost unbelievable reality that was trying to break into minds addled by fear, grief, and a lack of sleep. I know it sounds crazy, but He'd been seen, really, He'd been seen alive! And not at a distance; this wasn't a case of mistaken identity or wishful thinking. Hope, that had been all but extinguished just a few days ago as they'd witnessed His execution, was daring to well up once again in what remained of the incredulous band of friends. They'd seen some simply amazing stuff before; they'd been astonished on multiple occasions, but this? This was a completely different ball game! If this were to be true, it would change everything.

Some were more easily convinced than others, but after 6 weeks all doubt was gone, in fact, there were days when it had been almost like old times as the friends talked and ate together, yet more impossible happenings made possible, simply by His being there. They understood now that a time was coming soon, when He would be going home to his Father, but they'd seen enough to know that their lives would never be the same.

As it turned out, the whole world would never be the same!

📖 *"The good news that came to you is going out all over the world. It is bearing fruit everywhere by changing lives, just as it changed your lives from the day you first heard and understood the truth about God's wonderful grace." Colossians 1:6*

It's bin day ...

You know how it is – you've looked at it through the kitchen window for weeks, hoping that somehow it will miraculously disappear all by itself until one day you grasp the glaringly obvious: unless I go out and pull up all the rubbish myself it'll stay right where it is!

The spring flowers were lovely for a bit, but then they went up to seed, and then they died, and then they fell over and started rotting, and now they were rubbish. Looking at it while wishing it was somehow different hadn't helped, so this afternoon I pulled on a pair of gloves, armed myself with a garden fork and several rubbish bags, and made my way into the back garden. Now, feeling virtuous and ever so slightly stiff, I'm awaiting the homecoming of him who'd better be impressed by my efforts!

Back indoors, I find myself in reflective mood, perhaps because of all that bending over which seems to have got my brain going. You see, sometimes my life looks a bit like my back garden did a couple of hours ago - some of it growing well and looking good, but some of it rubbish. I can sigh, wishing it was different, or I can roll my sleeves up and make the choice to do something about it. The Bible says we have a responsibility to get rid of our own rubbish (Ephesians 4).

One more thing, underneath the tangled rottenness of yesterday's plants, I discovered some seedlings that were being smothered. They're what you call a bit leggy at the moment - stretching up through the deadness, trying to reach the light; but they're full of potential, looking for an opportunity to grow and flourish. I wonder what I might find in my heart once the rubbish is cleared? What has God planted there that is waiting to burst into life?

🙏 **Father, today I am making the choice to get rid of those things that spoil me, that prevent me from being the person You have made me to be. Give me the courage and determination to be thorough, not making excuses to keep the bits I find hard to remove, or the bits I secretly quite enjoy. Thank You that You have planted good seed in my heart; I ask that You would grow in me those things that bring You glory, the things that make me like You. Amen**

Obedience ...

As I sat uncomfortably in the badly decorated waiting area, I was reminded again of a lesson my parents taught me – "Do as you are told!"

There wasn't much to be joyful about in that room, but I heard God call me to thank and praise Him for something that I could see no prospect of receiving anytime soon. I have walked with God for long enough to know that when He prompts me to do something there is always a reason, so quietly I began a sentence thanking God and offering Him praise in this difficult situation. Before I reached the end of my sentence, a lady came through the door, and what we had been led to believe was extremely unlikely suddenly became a reality right there, right then.

Now, please understand me, I'm not saying that giving thanks for something you don't have will always produce the same instant result that I saw on this occasion, my experience tells me differently; but God has been speaking to me about the importance of obedience and what happened in the waiting room underlined the need for us to do what God tells us to do, even if, sometimes, it doesn't appear to make too much sense.

I have also been reminded recently of what happened when Mary, the mother of Jesus, saw a need and told a bunch of servants to "Do whatever Jesus tells you to do." They did, and the result was the first recorded miracle when Jesus turned gallons of ordinary water into top quality wine (John 2).

If you and I don't listen, if we don't pay attention, then we may miss what God is telling us. How often in our prayer times do we spend the entire time telling God what we want Him to do, without giving Him a chance to get a word in edgeways?

So, what was the last thing God told you to do? Have you done it yet?

"When someone comes to Me, listens to My teaching and then follows it, it's like a person building a house who digs deep and lays foundations on a solid rock. When the floodwaters rise and break against that house it stands firm because it is well build." Luke 6:47-48

Father, please forgive me for the times when I haven't responded to your voice. Help me to not only hear you, but to obey you.

Where do YOU find God?

Just give me a minute ...

Thanks. I needed that.

You see, life is full - too full. Time to meet with God, to talk to Him about the things that are breaking my heart right now is limited. What I love to do is walk, preferably in a leafy lane somewhere, and there I talk things over with my Father who loves me and cares about the things I care about. But when life kicks in and time goes out of the window, then what?

Then I remind myself that God does not live in the leafy lane, He lives in me. And where I am, He is, so I open my hurting heart to the God who loves me and I pray:

🙏 **Father, thank You that You will walk through today with me, going every place I go, seeing what I see, hearing what I hear. Breath in me and through me, bringing love and comfort to the people I meet, and to me.**

At just the right time ...

Do you think it is possible to think too much?

Are there questions we shouldn't ask?

Can we live contentedly knowing that there's stuff we will never know?

I guess if we knew everything, every answer to every question, there would be no need for faith, and the Bible says we can't please God without it.

In the Bible, at the end of Mark 6, right after Jesus had feed over 5000 people with a small boy's picnic, there's an amazing account of a long, windy night on a lake –

Jesus sent His disciples on ahead to row across the lake, known as the Sea of Galilee, while He went off alone to pray. It says that during the evening Jesus saw from the hillside that His friends were struggling because a strong wind had come up against them. The great news is that Jesus went to them, and the incredible and much argued over bit is that He even walked across the water to get to them!

But, the difficult bit for me is not that He walked on water, but that He waited until between 3 and 6 in the morning before He went to them. Sure, they were scared witless when they saw Him, and surprise surprise, the winds calmed down the minute He stepped into the boat. But why did He wait all that time? Knowing that they were finding it so hard, why did He wait so long before He came to them?

Then again, why did He not stop the wind blowing before He walked across the lake to them? His journey took Him through the same storm that they were battling. As Jesus approaches them and while the wind is still doing its worst, He speaks words of comfort,

 "Don't be afraid, it's Me, I'm here now." **Mark 6:50**

So, what are the winds threatening you? Are you worn out with the struggle?

Feeling hopelessly ill-equipped and perhaps even, from time to time, abandoned?

Don't be afraid, for this I know, at just the right time, He will come.

Time to move?

I wonder where your favourite place is? You know, that place where your heartbeat seems to gain momentum, or maybe, where it slows a little and a sense of peace settles over you like early morning dew.

As a little girl my favourite place was on the farm where my Dad and my Grandad worked. I would nestle into the clean bed of straw with the tiny calves stroking their velvety ears, and at feed time I would plunge my arm into a bucket of milk and allow them to suck on my fingers so that they would learn to drink. Their rough tongues seemed to drag my hand into their slobbery mouths almost up to my wrist!

The grown up me has a different favourite place, the majestic tranquillity of the Yorkshire Dales. Whenever I get the chance to return there, my throat tightens very slightly as the area seems to almost wrap itself around me, whispering, "Welcome back." I miss it when I'm not there and I hate leaving when it's time to come away. Winter or summer, it's always beautiful and no matter what the season, there's something unchanging about it.

Being creatures of habit, we took our children back many times, often to the same cottage, but last time we stayed there something had changed; I noticed it within minutes of us all tumbling out of the car ...

You'd think that a lump of rock the size of Ingleborough would be impossible to miss, an immovable object, a constant amidst all the changes that life throws at you. But as I stepped onto the balcony to inhale the clear air and let the view revive my soul I saw, with horror, that it had gone; Ingleborough was no longer visible. I instantly realised that it was because the trees in the wood the other side of the meadow had grown in the 3 years that had passed since I last stood in this spot. It wouldn't have happened suddenly of course, but inch by inch those trees had crept skywards, until one day, the mountain had apparently disappeared.

My family laughed at my dismay; but washing up at the cottage wouldn't be quite so much fun without the mountain to gaze at. The owner, though pleased to see us once again, didn't respond very positively to my suggestion that the trees be shortened either!

As I sat by the open window in the early stillness of the following morning, I pondered the lost view. Of course, Ingleborough was there as much this year as it had been for millennia; all I needed to do was come out from behind the trees and I would see it perfectly once again.

But it made me ask myself a question - Are there any "trees" obscuring my view of God right now?

He is every bit as much present as He has ever been, but sometimes, inch by inch, things can grow up and we can end up losing sight of Him. If you find that to be the case, then either it's time to move or else, maybe it's time to chop some trees down!

🙏 **Father in heaven, thank You that You remain steadfast and true from generation to generation. Help me to identify anything that may be threatening to obscure my view of You and give me wisdom so that I will know what to do about it. Amen**

Shhh ... listen

Some days life is like a millpond, all is calm.

Some days, life ploughs a course through torrential rain and angry waves.

Jesus' disciples were having one of those days - literally!

They started out anxious and ended up terrified, and then someone had a brainwave,

"Let's tell Jesus."

He'd been there all the time.

When Jesus spoke, awe replaced terror.

So, what is the storm that you are facing today?

Have you talked to Jesus, told Him about it? Remember, He's with you in the storm. What might He be saying that will change your fear to awe?

Shhh ... listen!

 "Let the peace of Christ rule in your hearts ..." **Colossians 3 v 15**

Lessons from Paris ...

The Arc de Triomph was indeed a magnificent building, but down at street level, the noise was deafening, the pace was frantic, the dust was choking and it was hard to see more than a few yards ahead of us for the crowds!

Almost 300 heart pounding, lung bursting, muscle aching stone steps later, we emerged into the morning sunshine that bathed the top of this glorious monument and all at once, everything changed. The noise faded into the background, the air cleared and the view across the city was breath-taking. From up here, it made much more sense - the tree-lined avenues, the way the great church of Sacre Coeur keeps watch over the entire city, it all looked so different.

And God spoke into our hearts.

We see life from street level so often, but God invites us to look at things from His perspective, to climb out of the dust and the noise of our own thinking and to let the Holy Spirit show us another way of seeing.

"God, make it down here where we are, like it is up there where You are." Matthew 6 v 9,10

And now for something completely different ...

It's raining! I know, I know - it's a good thing because the gardens need the rain and the runner beans will be so much better for it and it's been dry for days, well, weeks really so it's time we had some rain ... but I like the sunshine!

And I had to work all day today; hardly sat down and my legs ached at the end of the afternoon and when I got in, I had to get my own tea. And that wasn't easy because my mouth is sore and you can get fed up with soup and yoghurt after a while!

And then I noticed that those pesky red lily beetles have had all my lilies in the last few days, and these little bugs, they make SO much mess and the poor plants are ruined - again. The cat seems quite happy though, and so she should be considering the lengths I go to to get her to eat these days. I know she's old, but really, home cooked chicken with rice? She eats better than I do!

Enough! Enough! Sounds like I could grumble for England doesn't it?!

Do you ever find yourself sliding into grumbling mode, where nothing seems to be quite how you'd like it and even if they try (which obviously they don't seem to!) your family and friends cannot do anything right?

Then stop a minute; it's time for an attitude adjustment.

Instead of seeing all the things around you that justify your grumbling, look harder and uncover the things that you can be grateful for. Swap your moaning for thanksgiving, give out praise instead of criticism, and watch the atmosphere change.

"Oh, come, let us sing to the Lord! Give a joyous shout in honour of the Rock of our salvation! Come before Him with thankful hearts. Let us sing Him psalms of praise. For the Lord is a great God, the great King of all gods." Psalm 95:1-3

Father, please forgive me when I grumble about everything and everyone. Please create in me a thankful heart, always looking for the best in people rather than keeping count of their shortcomings. Make me more like You Jesus, Amen.

He who has ears to hear...

You can picture the scenario I'm sure - they're on the drag this morning, but there's something he needs to know before they leave for work . Over breakfast, in between checking the emails that come in via his I-phone, he reels off a few things that need to go on the shopping list for the weekend; she tries again to get his attention but the newspaper has gotten there first. Later, on the way into town in the car he doesn't seem to hear the increasingly urgent calling of his name over the manic ramblings of the DJ. If only he would listen.

Then, finally, and just in time, he sees it; ahead of them the road is blocked. He stops sharply but now he's frustrated and angry, "Why do these things always happen to me?"

The signs had gone up the night before, and she had been trying to point out the warnings and diversions for the last couple of miles, but he'd been talking to the office on his mobile and hadn't taken any notice. Now they were going to be late for work and apparently it was all her fault! "Why didn't you tell me?" He performs a hasty 3-point turn whilst ranting about potholes and the cuts in council budgets so he doesn't hear the reply to his question: "You weren't listening."

I wonder how often God tries to get our attention, wanting to tell us something? How often are we too busy or distracted to notice? And when our path is suddenly blocked, how often do we blame God for not guiding us another way? How often might He whisper, "I tried, but you weren't listening."

Life can be busy, and we know that sometimes the urgent can get in the way of the important. Why not step out of the fast lane for an hour or so; take time to connect with the God who loves you.

"Come to Me. Get away with Me and you'll recover your life ... Walk with Me, and work with Me – watch how I do it. Learn the unforced rhythms of grace." Matthew 11:28-29

Can't stay ...

Sorry, but now I've arrived I realise that I shouldn't be here at all. As I try to drag my mind away from the list of things I want to achieve today, the persistent, perhaps even nagging thought that I've been pushing to the back of my head all day surges forward and now, it sits full square in front of me: "I'm still waiting."

This isn't the drumming-my-fingers-on-the-table kind of waiting, but the craning-my-neck-watching-for-you-to-come-round-the-corner-any-minute-now kind of waiting.

It's not that I haven't thought about God today, I have. It's not that I haven't prayed today, I have. But when I dashed off to work early this morning, I told Him that I'd sit with Him when I got back; then I decided to go and do the Tesco shopping first. When I got home I woke my teenage son, visited a sick friend, stopped for a bite to eat, made plans for baking and ironing and gardening and answering emails and completing questionnaires and writing, before cooking dinner this evening - all good and noble things to do - but I can't help feeling that I've missed out today.

It's not that God was not with me when I was at work, He was. It's not that He wasn't watching over me as I shopped and visited and ate and got busy, He was. Yet my Father in heaven is waiting for me to turn my gaze in His direction, to put everything else down for a few minutes and to sit with Him so that I can hear Him more easily, because there are things He wants to say, things He wants me to know.

Incredibly, it's not just me that feels like I've missed out today.

🙏 Father, I've finished here now and I'm coming to sit with You. If there are things You want to say to me, I'll be listening. And if not, then it will be enough just to know that I am with You, and You are with me. Amen

The Living Word ...

If you could see the mess on my living room floor right now, you would understand why I am biting my tongue so as not to say anything! I have come away to the comparative order of the study while I decide what, if anything to say.

You see, words are powerful, and we must use them carefully. Already this week I have seen the power of words to crush a spirit, to degrade and belittle causing head and shoulders to be stooped. But, also this week, I've seen words build up and encourage, a chin lifted by the reminder of a happy memory and an affirmation temporarily forgotten.

God sets great store by words; Jesus is even known as the Living Word. Deuteronomy 8:3 says that we need God's words to be able to live, really live. In the New Testament, John tells of a tough time during Jesus' ministry when many decided that following Him was just too hard. Jesus asked His closest friends if they wanted to pull out too. Peter acted as spokesman and said, "Lord, who would we go to? You have the words that give eternal life."

Some days are, well, I was going to say tough, but for the days I'm thinking of, "tough" doesn't cover it. We look to God with pain-filled eyes and we struggle to find words to convey the desolation that we feel; but even then, we can find ourselves clinging to Him because ... where else can we go?

He still has the words that give eternal life.

And in a quiet moment, the God of all comfort can be heard to whisper:

"But now, this is what the Lord says: Don't be afraid, for I have redeemed you; I have called you by name; you are mine. When you pass through the waters, I will be with you; and when you have to cross deep rivers, they will not sweep over you. When you walk through the fire, you will not be burned; the flames will not set you ablaze. For I am the Lord, your God, the Holy One of Israel, your Saviour ... you are precious in My sight and I love you. Don't be afraid, for I am with you." Isaiah 43:1-5

Walking in truth - not so silly?

I loved my Grandad ... and he was the silliest man I ever knew! He had the most amazing repertoire of silly songs and was known to sing the words, "Bill Smith knew my father; father knew Bill Smith" to the tune Onward Christian Soldiers, at the top of his voice, all the way from his house to the beach - a distance of almost two miles - right through the town centre. To us grandchildren it was utterly hilarious - if slightly embarrassing sometimes!

This was my favourite though; sung to the tune of Yankee Doodle it went like this, "Our house is a semi-detached, it says so on the leases; if it wasn't for the other one, ours would fall to pieces!"

My Grandad had lots of sayings too and the one that has stuck, and which my own children now refer to as "Doing a Grandad Watts" is this – "I promise to tell the truth, the whole truth, and anything but the truth."

And how easy it is too - to not tell a lie, but to not tell the truth either. The Bible tells us that Jesus is Truth, and that the enemy of our souls is called The Father of Lies, so how come we still don't get how important this is?

One of the original Ten Commandments given to Moses for the fledgling nation of Israel was to not tell lies about each other and in Colossians 3 where Paul is giving instructions to new Christians in the early days of the church, he tells them, **"Do not lie to each other. You have left your old sinful life and the things you did before. You have begun to live the new life, in which you are being made new and are becoming like the One who made you."**

In his letter to the church at Ephesus, Paul says that living in the truth is part of God's protection package for His people; failure to speak, to live and to believe the truth makes us vulnerable and causes damage to others and to us.

King David wanted to know how to remain close to God, constantly. And the answer?

"Walk with integrity, do what is righteous, and speak the truth within your heart." Psalm 15

Father, please forgive me for the times that I tell a version of the truth; for the times when I exaggerate a story for effect; for using half-truths and lies of various colours to get myself out of a tight spot or to claim credit that I don't deserve. You are Truth, and when I reflect You and who You are, You protect and safeguard me from the enemy. Fill me with Your Holy Spirit, and give me the courage to stand up for truth. And when I come to You? Help me not to pretend to You either, but to come just as I am, certain of Your love. In Jesus' name, Amen.

One morning, not so long ago ...

It was 6.30 in the morning and there wasn't a breath of wind, nor a cloud in the sky. The sun was climbing above the sea, which was not only completely calm, but rather unusually, almost blue. As I crunched my way up the beach, I let out a long sigh, and drank in the magnificence of it all. God was in this place.

After I'd walked for a bit, I noticed on the pebbles a couple of feet above the water line, an up-turned starfish, still wriggling those amazing little tentacles that cover the underside of each of their 5 stumpy legs. "Poor little chap!" I picked him up gently and tossed him back into the sea. A few minutes later, another and then another, all returned to the sea.

But I hadn't set out at that hour of the morning to rescue starfish, so I sat for a while, pondering and praying, thinking of those I know and love who are struggling, hurting, sick and sad. I sat for some time, for the list is a long one.

Eventually, comforted by time spent in such a beautiful place alone with my Father in heaven, I turned back the way I'd come. Once again, I found starfish after starfish, all washed up and in need of help.

"He needed me!"

I think I said it out loud as I tossed yet another back, and then it struck me. It wasn't ME he needed - it was the sea. Had I carried them all for long, it would have been no help whatsoever. No, it was the sea they needed, I was just there to help them on their way, to bring the two together if you like.

And then I thought of those I'd been praying for, of those I'd wept over, of those I was trying to carry - and I knew, that in the end, it's not ME they need, it's Jesus. I don't have all the answers, He does. I can't be with them all the time, He can. I'm not their healer, He is. My job is to bring them before God, to bring the two together - to intercede.

🙏 **Father, I bring to You those who are struggling, hurting, sick and sad, and I ask that You would carry them. The load is too much for me and anyway, it's not actually me that they need, it's You.**

Change? What change?!

Life is full of changes. Sometimes a change can be an upgrade, and sometimes we're not so sure.

Like my precious little granddaughter: not long ago I could sit her in the middle of the living room floor with a heap of toys knowing that when I came back from the bathroom a few minutes later she would still be there. Not any more!

Like my son's bedroom floor: at one time I could barely walk from one side of his room to the other for fear of what I may inadvertently stand on amongst the secondary floor coverings. Now the carpet has been revealed once again, the midnight TV silenced, and the fridge contents remain in the fridge while I am out!

Change is a good thing; change provides the opportunity to discover for ourselves the truth that while pretty much everything else may change, God never does. By which I don't mean that He will say and do exactly the same things no matter what the situation, oh no, neither does it mean that our experiences of God will be the same in any given set of circumstances.

It's not God's actions that are unchangeable, it's His character.

He is love - always.
He is faithful - always.
He speaks the truth - always.
He is good - always.
He does what is right - always.

He is the God of all comfort, the Good Shepherd, the source of peace and strength and courage and joy beyond reason.
So, how are you with the changes that are happening in your world?

📖 *"Trust in the Lord with all your heart; do not depend on your own understanding. Seek His will in all you do, and He will show you which path to take." Proverbs 3:5-6*

🙏 **Heavenly Father, I thank You for the knowledge that You will hold me firm and secure in this season of change. You have promised not to leave me, and You always keep Your promises. You are unchanging; You were the same yesterday as You are today, and You'll be the same again tomorrow. You are an amazing God!**

Still time ...

You know how every now and then you get to witness something special, an intimate moment shared by others that leaves you feeling a bit like an intruder, and yet privileged to have been there all at the same time? Well that was me one afternoon not so long ago, and the memory will live long in my heart.

Cradled gently by the hospice bed in which he slept, a frail, elderly husband woke briefly. His wife, attentive to his every move, heaved herself out of her chair and bending tenderly over him asked if he would like her to read. Eventually a faint nod was detected and slowly, deliberately, as she had done every day for many weeks, she opened her Bible at Isaiah 41:10

"So do not fear, for I am with you;
do not be dismayed, for I am your God.
I will strengthen you and help you;
I will uphold you with My righteous right hand."

Then they both closed their eyes and together they thanked God for the wonderful truth of those words before praying, as they did every day... for their children, now grandparents themselves.

At the end of the bed, in that most sacred place, silent tears flowed as it dawned on me that the prayers of this precious man would soon be silenced.

There is a baton to be passed on; you and I still have time to pray. There is work yet to be done as we watch and wait for the purposes of God to be fulfilled in our families, our churches, our communities and among the nations.

God grant me the faithfulness of this mother and father as I pray for my own children; may I never grow weary of lifting them up to You. And may Your kingdom come, Your will be done on earth, as it is in heaven. Amen

Waiting ...

It's a funny thing ... waiting. Waiting can be filled with excitement or filled with fear. Waiting can mean everyone's in this together, or it can mean an intense loneliness. Waiting can leave us energised, or waiting can suck us dry.

I guess it all depends what you're waiting for, and who you're waiting with. Waiting can leave us torn, as for one bit of me the waiting is a deep longing, whilst for another bit of me the same waiting can seem more like dread.

... and God's word to me today? "I am with you in the waiting."

... and suddenly the waiting is not the focus, for I know with absolute certainty that I am not waiting alone.

... and I am reminded of something I have said before and still believe with all my heart,

"At just the right time, He will come."

"The Lord is my light and my salvation—whom shall I fear?
The Lord is the stronghold of my life—of whom shall I be afraid?
One thing I ask from the Lord, this only do I seek:
that I may dwell in the house of the Lord all the days of my life, to gaze on the beauty of the Lord and to seek Him in His temple.
For in the day of trouble He will keep me safe in His dwelling; He will hide me in the shelter of His sacred tent and set me high upon a rock.
My heart says of You, "Seek his face!" Your face, Lord, I will seek...
Wait for the Lord; be strong and take heart and wait for the Lord."
From Psalm 27

In the valley ...

"Don't be afraid; I'm here with you."

God has said this to me on numerous occasions throughout the last 12 months and this week I have experienced a sense of the presence of God that has proved again the awesome truth of these words.

There are times when we travel the lush green paths of the hilltop, enjoying the warmth of the sun on our faces and a lightness in our spirits; but at other times we are called to walk the arid, dusty paths of the Valley of the Shadow.

Whichever path we find ourselves on, God walks with us.

Fear attempts to rob us of faith, but as we hold fast, as we chose to trust the God of all comfort, we find again that God is more than able to strengthen us, to give us courage, to enable us to find His footprints on the journey that we have been forced to take.

Even in the valley, God is still God and He is to be praised because, just as our joy cannot add to Him, so He is undiminished by our sadness.

I don't know what kind of terrain your journey is passing through right now, but I do know that there is no path so dark that He cannot travel with you.

"You, LORD, are my shepherd. I will never be in need. You let me rest in fields of green grass. You lead me to streams of peaceful water, and You refresh my life. You are true to Your name, and You lead me along the right paths. I may walk through valleys as dark as death, but I won't be afraid. You are with me, and Your shepherd's rod makes me feel safe. You treat me to a feast, while my enemies watch. You honour me as Your guest, and You fill my cup until it overflows. Your kindness and love will always be with me each day of my life, and I will live forever in Your house, LORD." Psalm 23

Forwards, not backwards ...

Has your body clock adjusted to the end of British Summer Time yet? I'm not keen on the dark evenings if I'm honest, but hey ho, it'll soon be spring! Perhaps it's a sign of my advancing years, but when the clocks went back last weekend, it really did feel like it was 10 when it was only 9 on Sunday evening, but by Monday morning at 7 it felt like it was 6 instead of 8! Confused? Me too!

Ever wished you could really turn the clocks back? Not just an hour in the autumn, but a day, a week, 6 months, or years maybe? What would you do if you could go back in time?

Some of us would go back to a day when we were particularly happy or fulfilled and re-live it over and over again; some of us would revisit a moment of deep regret in order to right a wrong; some of us would try with the benefit of hindsight to sidestep an event or a set of circumstances that led to pain or injury of body, mind or spirit.

Something I have learned is that while our past will certainly have shaped our present, it doesn't have to limit our future. Instead of wishing that we could go backwards, we must press on, moving forwards to take hold of all that God has been preparing for us. In the Bible, a man called Paul understood this and wrote in a letter to Christians in the city of Phillippi:

"But one thing I do, forgetting what is behind and straining towards what is ahead, I press on towards the goal to win the prize for which God has called me heavenwards in Christ Jesus."

If we continue to hold onto the past with both hands, we will be unable to reach out and take hold of the adventure that is a future with God.

Father in heaven, I give to You all my yesterdays, thanking You that they have brought me to this point today, where I am ready to accept Your invitation to continue my life's journey with You. I don't know what lies ahead, but I do know that You have plans for me that are rooted in Your love and goodness. I choose to trust You with my past, and with my future. Amen

Serve ...

You know how sometimes, it's not the job that needs doing that's the issue, it's who it needs doing for? Like on a day when you're weary and a bit off colour and your other half hints that a cuppa would be nice and you ignore the hint hoping that they'll go get it themselves; but when someone pops round unexpectedly, you leap out of your seat, rush to the kitchen to put the kettle on protesting that it's no trouble at all! Maybe there's an elderly neighbour who's lonely and unwell, and you would call in but there's just no time for house calls in your busy week; until a new young family move in three doors down and suddenly you find that there's time to be neighbourly after all.

Serving others costs - not necessarily money, but time, energy, emotion. It's easy to be kind to those who will be grateful, to those who will sing your praise, to those who will be kind in return. But how do you motivate yourself to serve the unloved? There's a reason why they're unloved, right?

📖 *"Then the King will say to those on His right, 'Enter, you who are blessed by My Father! Take what's coming to you in this kingdom. It's been ready for you since the world's foundation. And here's why:*
I was hungry and you fed Me,
I was thirsty and you gave Me a drink,
I was homeless and you gave Me a room,
I was shivering and you gave Me clothes,
I was sick and you stopped to visit,
I was in prison and you came to Me.'
"Then those 'sheep' are going to say, 'Master, what are you talking about? When did we ever see You hungry and feed You, thirsty and give You a drink? And when did we ever see You sick or in prison and come to You?' Then the King will say, 'I'm telling the solemn truth: Whenever you did one of these things to someone overlooked or ignored, that was Me—you did it to Me.'
"Then He will turn to the 'goats,' the ones on His left, and say, 'Get out, worthless goats! You're good for nothing but the fires of hell. And why? Because—
I was hungry and you gave Me no meal,
I was thirsty and you gave Me no drink,
I was homeless and you gave Me no bed,
I was shivering and you gave Me no clothes,
Sick and in prison, and you never visited.'
"Then those 'goats' are going to say, 'Master, what are You talking about? When did we ever see You hungry or thirsty or homeless or shivering or sick or in prison and didn't help?' "He will answer them, 'I'm telling the solemn truth: Whenever you failed to do one of these things to someone who was being overlooked or ignored, that was Me—you failed to do it to Me.'
Matthew 25:34-45

🙏 Dearest Lord Jesus, You were willing to pay the cost in order to serve us; You left, not an arm chair, but a throne in heaven so that You could show us how to serve one another. King of Glory, You became a servant, willing to die, so that we could be with You one day. Thank You that Your grace is always available to me when an opportunity for service comes my way. May I choose to serve as You would serve, on Your behalf, in Your name. Amen

Wait for it ...

I've been busy in the garden again! It was my birthday last week and I received a shrub for the front border - a forsythia. We had one at home when I was little, and I've always loved the bright yellow flowers, and now I have one of my own; another reason to look forward to spring! At the moment, however, it looks like a bunch of brown twigs with the odd leaf here and there.

It has reminded me of prayer and asking God for things. Sometimes when we ask for something, what we get looks nothing like the thing we were hoping for - a bit like my bunch of brown twigs. But if we plant what we receive, water it in with our prayers and wait on God then, in time, very often, that bunch of twigs will blossom and a thing of beauty will emerge.

It is true that asking does not always produce the result we had in mind, but it is also true that God is more willing to give than we imagine, that His generosity and love know no bounds, that He is able to turn something dry and ugly into a source of joy and celebration.

"Ask, and keep on asking; seek, and keep on seeking; knock and keep on knocking." Matthew 7:7

Father, please forgive me that I give up so easily, that I judge Your response to my prayers by my own standards. I know You are teaching me what it means to persevere, teaching me to rely on You and Your grace. Thank you that You are my Father in heaven, not a method that either works or doesn't. Thank You that there is potential in every situation for Your name to be honoured and Your Kingdom to be established. Please help me to live well through the dry times, looking ahead with a sense of purpose and confidence as I trust in You. Amen

Just another juggling ball?

So much to do, so little time! If you ever find out how to be in two places at once, please let me in on the secret; I've tried, really I have, but no. Unless I multitask, and let's be honest, even us girls find it difficult to multitask well, then I will have to continue to make choices about what I do first, or next.

I've never been much of a juggler either; my hand eye co-ordination is just not up to it. Catching just one ball has always been hard enough for me, never mind trying to throw and catch more than one all at the same time!

I have choices to make when I pray too: should I pray while driving to the supermarket today, or while I do the ironing? Perhaps I'll pray while digging up potatoes, or sitting on the train. I've done all of the above, and they're all good, but you know what? Some things work better when I give them my full attention.

I can chat to my hubby while he's scrolling through his phone messages or watching the telly; he can tell me about his day while I'm straining the veg and stirring the gravy, but meaningful conversation works best when we sit together, or walk together giving each other our undivided attention; when we take time to listen with our eyes; when our body language says, "Nothing is more important to me right now than being here with you."

God loves us, in fact He's devoted to us and so I'm sure that He's pleased whenever we're thinking of Him, even if it is at the same time as everything else. But there are times when He wants to capture our full attention, to know that being with Him is the most important thing we have on right now; times when we would catch His whisper, if only we were to stop long enough to listen.

🙏 **Father, thank You for loving me in the here and now. Thank you that You constantly watch over me, that Your ear is always turned towards me. I know You are with me in the busyness of each day, but please help me today to make the time to turn my heart towards You, to make being with You the most important thing. Amen**

Where are You?

Let me tell you about a man called Job; some would say he was the unluckiest man that ever lived! At first, he was wealthy whichever way you looked at it - he had a great relationship with God, a large family that loved him and each other, a thriving business and the respect of his community. Life was good.

But it all went wrong. In a single day Job learned that his business had collapsed following a hostile take-over and a so-called natural disaster; his employees had been attacked and most of them killed. While he was still trying to get his head round what had just happened, he got the news that all ten of his children had lost their lives in a freak storm. Not long after that terrible day, Job was taken ill and he suffered horribly, so much so that when his friends popped round to see him, they hardly recognised him and could find nothing to say for days. To cap it all, when they finally found their voices, they added to his pain by telling him over and over again that it must all have been his fault somehow.

But despite everything, Job stayed true to his faith in God. He didn't understand why all this had happened to him and his family, but he still trusted God. At one point he made this amazing statement:

"I look for God in the east, but He is not there; I go to the west, but I cannot perceive Him; I look to the north to see Him at work but I cannot, and neither is He to be found in the south.
But He knows where I am ..." Job 23:8-10

Job searched desperately, hoping to find a reason for all the things that had happened to him, but none was found.

What do you see as you look around you? Do you see evidence of God at work in your health, your family, your business, your community, or, like Job, are you struggling to find God at work whichever direction you look in?

You may not know where God is right now ... but believe me, He knows where you are.

Father, when the silence of unanswered prayers threatens to overwhelm me, let the knowledge that You not only know where I am, but are holding tightly onto me bring comfort and strength as I wait. Amen

To start the day ...

So many choices first thing on a Monday morning ...!

Jump out of bed and make a flying start to the week or sneak a few more minutes and delay the inevitable? The black jumper with the beige skirt or the blue jumper with the black trousers? And breakfast, lamb in jelly or fish in gravy? (No, not my breakfast, the cat's breakfast!)

Having decided on fat free peach yoghurt for my own breakfast I find I must now choose my attitude to today. Will I trust my heavenly Father in every situation, or try to prove that I can manage perfectly well without Him? And what kind of a prayer will I pray before I head off into the busyness?

Ah, that's a good question. What do I really want to say to God this morning? Where can I find the words I want to say?

"Hear me, Lord, and answer me, for I am poor and needy.
Guard my life, for I am faithful to You; save Your servant who trusts in You.
You are my God; have mercy on me, Lord, for I call to You all day long.
Bring joy to your servant, Lord, for I put my trust in You.
You, Lord, are forgiving and good, abounding in love to all who call to You.
Hear my prayer, Lord; listen to my cry for mercy.
When I am in distress, I call to You, because You answer me.
Among the gods there is none like You, Lord; no deeds can compare with Yours.
All the nations You have made will come and worship before You, Lord; they will bring glory to Your name.
For You are great and do marvellous deeds; You alone are God.
Teach me Your way, Lord, that I may rely on Your faithfulness; give me an undivided heart, that I may fear Your name.
I will praise You, Lord my God, with all my heart;
I will glorify Your name forever.
For great is Your love toward me ..." Psalm 86

Guilty as charged?

Have you ever been accused?

"Accused of what?" I hear you say. Oh, I don't know, accused of not listening, or not caring maybe; accused of eating the last piece of chocolate cake, of making a mess or not clearing up? Or perhaps you've been accused of working too hard or too late; of getting too involved, or of being hard-hearted?

I have been accused, on more than one occasion, of being a bit of a mother hen! And in some ways, I guess it's true. I have been known to be fiercely protective of those I care about. I love to nurture and to watch others grow. A strong desire to help others feel safe has been a part of who I am for a long time.

But that's ok isn't it? Well yes, I think so, but this morning as I was reading the Bible something struck me with some force, making me question the way I often pray for those I find myself watching over.

In Acts 4 the story is told of how Peter and John were in big trouble with the authorities because they were teaching the people about Jesus, both by what they said and what they did. The religious leaders felt threatened by these ordinary men whose words and lives were being used by God to bring truth to the people, so they had Peter and John arrested and thrown into prison overnight while they tried to work out how to stop them talking about Jesus anymore.

Now my instinct at this point in the story is to look for a way to keep these guys safe, to pray for their protection, so it is with some relief that I notice the church of the day were on the same page as me - they got everyone together to pray.

But wait, they didn't pray for protection and safety for these men, they prayed for boldness for them so that their words and their lives wouldn't stop telling the truth about Jesus (Acts 4:29-30). Wasn't that rather dangerous? A little foolhardy even? I mean, Peter and John had already been arrested, imprisoned and threatened. Would God really answer a prayer that might result in His followers having to face yet more difficult situations? Seems He would!

"After they prayed, the place where they were meeting was shaken. And they were all filled with the Holy Spirit and spoke the word of God boldly." Acts 4:31

So now I have to think about how I should pray for those who have already found, and are following Jesus. Should I be asking God to simply keep them safe? Or is it time to ask instead that God would enable His people to speak His word "with great boldness"?

Nothing wrong here ...

How odd would it be if, when I walk into church on Sunday morning, everyone was examining their chair closely to see if it were safe to sit on? I mean, how would you know? If chairs were unreliable things then chivalrous men would dash ahead of well-dressed ladies and Mum's would hold back their wriggling offspring until the chair had been thoroughly checked out and passed as fit for purpose by the overstretched resident health and safety officer!

For years I've heard our attitude to the dependable chair used as an example of what it means to put our trust in God, and in truth, there is some merit in this comparison. But it struck me yesterday that a chair can only do one thing, it just sits there, so that you can, well, just sit there. It treats everyone the same, it does dependability, but it doesn't do creativity, adaptability or individuality. A chair doesn't have feelings, opinions or make choices.

You're wondering where I'm going with this, I can tell!

Several years ago, when I was praying long and hard about something very important, a wise man showed me a verse from the Bible. I had told him that I was trusting God to do what I was asking Him to do and this is what the verse said:

 "Will not the Judge of all the earth do what's right?" **Genesis 18:25**

Pray with all your heart, but know this - one size doesn't fit all with God.

He knows what is right, according to His own great mercy and love.

All His ways are just, always.

Trust Him completely, like you do a chair, without giving it a second thought, but be assured that even though things don't always turn out the way you'd planned, or hoped they would, God can do no wrong.

Heavenly Father, there are plenty of times when I don't understand why things are the way things are, but the Bible shows me who You are and so I chose again to trust You. You gave the life of Your only Son for me, and proved beyond question that You are for me and not against me. Thank You that You know me completely, and that You are not unmoved by the situations that I face; thank You that as You hear and answer all the prayers that I am praying, You will do what is right. Amen

It is well with my soul ...

On this particular afternoon, I found myself sitting on my favourite beach, while the rain lashed down and the angry wind fought against me. The waves smashing the stony beach over and over again reflected the relentless pain in my heart as I faced a storm in life that seemed more than equal to the gale which now engulfed me. As rain and tears mingled on my cheeks, the words of an old hymn came to mind:

"When peace like a river attendeth my way,
When sorrows like sea billows roll,
Whatever my lot, You have taught me to know
It is well, it is well with my soul."

And somehow, in that moment, I knew it to be true. God met me as I sat on the beach in the storm and spoke peace to my battered heart. For a time, whilst the tempest continued to roar on the outside, on the inside, calm was restored.

There was a man in the Bible who was having a seriously tough time, and it tells us that God spoke to him "out of the storm".

And this I know with all my heart – whatever you are facing, whatever kind of storm you find yourself in, be it sickness, doubt, loss, fear, debt, or anything else, you need not face it alone.

For I have learned, that the God of peace inhabits the storm.

Printed in Great Britain
by Amazon